Prayers

FOR LIFE'S

Ordinary

AND

Extraordinary

Moments

Compiled and Edited by

MARY LOU REDDING

UPPER
ROOM BOOKS®
NASHVILLE

Cover design and interior layout: Bruce Gore / www.gorestudio.com

ISBN 978-0-8358-1089-0
Printed in the United States of America

CONTENTS

THE CRY FOR JUSTICE

LOSS AND GRIEF

IN UNCERTAIN TIMES

ASKING FOR HEALING

FACING OUR OWN AND OTHERS' IMPERFECTIONS

SPIRITUAL SEARCHING

GRATITUDE FOR ORDINARY MIRACLES

INTRODUCTION

Hanging in the office of a former boss of mine was a poster that read something like this:

> An all-purpose prayer for
> when life is almost more
> than you can stand
> and you're about to be pulled under
> and no one seems to care
> and you don't know what to ask:
>
> HELP!

Can prayer really be as simple as a single word? At times, absolutely. Bringing the good and the bad of our lives to God in prayer sometimes seems simple and completely natural. We're able to empty out what stirs in our heart as easily and directly as we'd talk to our oldest friend in the world, someone with whom we have to hide nothing and explain little. But at other times, words just won't come. We can't find a way to express our feelings and concerns that helps us let go of them, or a way to talk about our joys that does them justice.

When that happens, it's not a failing on our part. Paul wrote in his letter to the Romans, "When we do not know how to pray . . . " He didn't say "*if* we don't know how." It's not a matter of *if* but of *when*. So *when* we can't find the words, God offers us help—sometimes, as Paul said, through the Holy Spirit praying on our behalf, and sometimes through other believers whose words carry us into God's presence.

The prayers in this collection are an attempt to be that group of fellow believers and friends for all who pick up the book. I invited people who work with me to reflect on their concerns and write prayers that reflect real life. I think you'll see that they did. I included a list of the names of those who contributed prayers for this book, but the individual prayers don't carry anyone's name. Not identifying the writers reminds us that these prayers might speak for any one of us at some point in our lives. We invite you to use the headings that organize this collection to find prayers for times when you need someone to help you pray.

Being able to pray is a privilege and a gift. Use this collection of prayers for the times you need someone to help you say what you want to say to God.

MARY LOU REDDING
Nashville, Tennessee
Spring 2011

FOR THE
People We Love

Thanksgiving for a Wise Friend

Dear God,
thank you for my wise friend and our recent
    conversation.
He really helped me sort through what I was
    struggling with.
It seemed to come as a word from you to ease my soul.
I am so grateful you have placed this person in my life.
Please continue to protect and guide him
and to give richly of your wisdom and your Spirit.
Teach me to let your Spirit come through me
as easily as it seems to come through him,
and use me to touch others in whatever way you choose.
I pray in the spirit of Christ,
whom you used so incredibly
and who showed us how to love our friends. *Amen.*

Thanksgiving for the Witness of an Elder

O God, today I give thanks for an elder
who has known me from my birth and loved me
     "just because."
She has shown me the fruit of the Spirit through the
     way she lives.
I give thanks for this friend, for the faithfulness in
     her life.
Knowing her makes me want to provide
a similar image to those who know me.
Thank you for the ways she blesses my life,
the lives of those in her congregation, and her family.
Use this opportunity to open my eyes
to the fruit of the Spirit lived out in others around me.
Thank you, loving God, for revealing yourself to us
through the lives of others. *Amen.*

When One We Love Is in Distress

Comforting God, my loved one is hurting,
and it feels like there is nothing I can do to ease
    the pain.
It's hard to watch this struggle.
The words I say seem lame and unhelpful.
You are the one who can unravel the mess,
show the way, heal the wounds.
Help me turn my loved one over to your gentle,
    loving care.
In hope and gratitude I pray. *Amen.*

At a Family Meal

Dear Lord, thank you for this meal
and for this gathering of people we love.
Bless everyone who had a part in growing the food,
preparing it, and bringing it to this table.
May each of us serve you to our fullest ability
and be strong witnesses of what it means
to live as your children. *Amen.*

When We Are Far Apart

Loving God,
we love others because you first loved us.
And it's hard when our loved ones are far from us.
When the people we love are far from us physically,
help us make the extra effort to stay close across
the miles.
When the people we love are far from us emotionally,
help us find words to say the right thing at the
right time.
When the people we love are far from us spiritually,
help us express our faith and our love for you.
Thank you for loving us so that we can love others.
In Christ's name we pray. *Amen.*

For an Unbelieving Child

Father God, thank you for your unconditional love
for each of your children.
I pray today especially for my child
who says he doesn't believe in you.

Lord, help my child struggling with cynicism
    and despair.
I believe that doubt is part of the faith journey.
Please send a sensitive soul to encourage my child—
someone who will say words to gently point
this one I love so much toward you.

Loving God, I lift up _____ to you.
Though it is difficult, I release my child to you,
trusting you to continue to work in his life.
Help me to let go and trust
that the seeds of faith I helped to plant will take root
and that my child will grow in the sunlight of your love.

Thank you, dear God, for hearing and acting.
I am grateful that you love this child
much more than I ever could,
and that though I must let go, you never will. *Amen.*

Gratitude for Good Friends

Loving God,
I am grateful today for good friends.
I thank you for those who
somehow know when I need their support
and understand how to step in
to do or say just what I need.
I am amazed when this happens—
and at how often it happens!
When I am grieving a loss large or small,
they know just what to say to comfort my soul.
When I am hurting from an injustice,
they can put the situation in perspective for me.
When I am angry, they can help me find balance.
When I am joyful, they celebrate with me.
My heart overflows with gratitude
for their presence in my life.
Thank you for them. *Amen.*

Thanksgiving for a Healing Friendship

Mender of every broken heart,
when I needed healing from deep hurt,
it didn't come easily or quickly.
I am so glad you sent someone to help me.
My hurt was so deep I couldn't even pray.
My heart and my lips went silent.
But your healing touch came through my friend.
She heard my cries. She saw my tears.
She reached out to me with your love and patience
to help healing begin.
You gave her the will and the words to pray for me
when I couldn't express my pain or name what I needed.
I know you put her in my life to be your healing touch.
And my prayer now, God, is that I can live my thanks
by walking a healing path with someone else.
Help me to be present, quiet, and faithful,
the kind of friend who embodies your will to heal.
May I be to others what my friend has been to me.
Amen.

Facing the Memory Loss of a Loved One

O God, today she didn't know me.
And it broke my heart to see her struggle to remember.
She looked so sad.

I got so angry when the others said,
"You know who this is, Mom. Of course you do."
I wanted to yell, "Leave her alone! Don't make her
    feel bad!"
I know they were only trying to help us feel better.
I'm sorry for my ugly thoughts toward them.

It is hard to know what to say and do; I feel so angry!
This disease has stolen her laughter,
her sense of humor—and now her bond with me.
I know that when she walks with you in eternity,
our ties to one another will all be restored,
and she will remember how much she is loved.
'Til then, Lord, help me, help all of us, to be patient.
Give us loving words to say.
Help us not to cause more pain.
Most of all, comfort her and assure her of your love.
Don't let her be afraid or feel alone,
and comfort us too. *Amen.*

For Reconciliation after Causing Pain

Lord of all, you have called us
to love our neighbors and our enemies.
I have strayed from your commandment
and sinned against you in the way
I have dealt with this relationship.
I have spoken harsh words and thought only of myself.
I have preferred my way,
not your gentle way of love and forgiveness.
I have caused hurt and sadness and resentment.
Forgive me, Lord, and help me to swallow my pride.
Help me to humbly ask forgiveness
and to take the first step toward reconciliation.
Strengthen me to do all I can
to restore the relationship that I have broken
and to relieve this distress.
Grant your grace and love as we communicate,
so that your peace may reign in our lives.
In Jesus' name I pray. *Amen.*

Struggling to Forgive

Jesus, you gave us some commandments
that are really tough to obey.

I'm struggling with not offering a gift at the altar
if you remember that a brother or sister
has something against you.
You said we should first be reconciled to our brother or
sister, and then come and offer our gift.*

Lord, I've been angry with _____ for a long time.
I'm still not sure I've totally forgiven.
How do we reconcile? It's been so long. What can I do?
Maybe this is just the way things are . . .
    and may remain.

God, please forgive me
for the times I've failed to forgive others.
Have mercy on me for not even recognizing when I've
    wronged someone.
And please help me to continue to love, even from afar,
until healing comes to both of us. *Amen.*

*See Matthew 5:23-24.

Birthdays

AND

Milestones

❧

Birth of a Grandchild

Loving Parent God,
I need patience.
It seems like such a long time
since we heard that our grandchild was on the way.
Now we are in the final weeks of waiting—
waiting to see whether the baby is healthy,
waiting to see who she looks like,
waiting to see how much she weighs,
waiting to see the parents' faces when she finally arrives,
waiting to hold this baby in our arms for the first time,
waiting to be there and to help,
waiting to share in the parents' joy,
Loving God, I need patience. *Amen.*

On Adopting a Child

Loving God, today we give thanks
for the biological mother of our child.
We know that this has been a difficult time in her life.
Giving up this child is perhaps the hardest decision
she will ever make.
Lord, comfort her with knowing
that we have loved and treasured
her child since the first time we laid eyes on him
and that we will keep on loving him.

We are honored to parent this child.
Help us always to be loving and caring parents
who live our faith in you before this child every day.
And show us, Lord, the right time to let our child know
that his mother made the sacrifice of placing him
        for adoption
as an act of love and to give opportunities she was not
        able to provide.
May the way we live and parent every day show
our gratitude for your gift of love given us in this child.
Amen.

First Day of Kindergarten

Lord, as we walk hand in hand
down this unfamiliar hallway,
let my child be met by leaders who
create a safe environment for learning.
Let her be met by a teacher who will love her
and see in her the gifts that I see.
Let her meet classmates who will befriend her.
Let her enter the school with the desire to learn.
Let her enter the classroom with joy and excitement.
Help her make friends by being the kind of friend Jesus
    taught us to be.
And, Lord, as I walk out of the school without her hand
    in mine,
fill me with the assurance that your hand holds
    hers firmly,
and that you'll never let go.
In the name of Jesus, who welcomed the children.
Amen.

The Empty Nest

O Lord, what do I do now?
There's a huge hole in my heart.
I knew this day was coming; I thought I was prepared.
But when my child walked away without either of us
knowing when we'd see each other's face again,
I thought I'd die.

You know how I worry;
some days, I have trouble just getting out of bed.
Thank you for sustaining me.
In time, may I learn to love the quiet instead of dread it.
Thank you for opportunities to do things for which
there was never time when the house was so busy.

Thank you for the blessing of this child.
Give me the grace to let him go out on his own,
trusting him to make his own decisions
and to learn from his mistakes as I learned from mine.
And help me and my child forge a new relationship that
honors our differences and opens the door
to valuing each other even more than before.
Help us to be not just parent and child
but friends as well. *Amen.*

At the Wedding of My Firstborn

O Lord, how did this day arrive so fast?

I can still see the curly-haired toddler riding a toy car.
I see that little girl in her serene face now.
She is standing up there in front of God, the minister,
and the man who will be her husband.

Oh, and Lord, he's about to become my son-in-law!
Guide me in this new relationship.
I want to trust that you know what is ahead.
Help me to listen and to love.

I struggle to release my child to her new life,
knowing that my relationship with her will never
    be the same.
But there is always the chance that it could be
    even better.

I breathe a prayer of blessing for this new couple,
    and I am happy.
Thank you, Lord, for being with us on this special day.
Amen.

Lord, I'm Thirty

Dear God,
I used to think that my parents and their generation
just didn't realize how much I had to offer.
I protested: "They don't understand.
They're too old. Times change. Why can't they?
If they'd bother to ask me,
I'd tell them how things ought to be."

When I was young,
I knew what my future would be like:
"By the time I'm thirty,
I'll make good money, travel, live in a nice place.
Maybe I'll even think about starting a family."

But, God, time has passed, and now I'm . . . thirty.
I'm thirty—and I have nothing to show for it!
I'm THIRTY, and it's nothing like I imagined.
Jesus, I'm thirty; help me figure out what to do now.
I'm . . . listening. *Amen.*

For a "Zero" Birthday

Well, God, today is another big one—
one of those birthdays that ends with a zero.
I can't believe I'm here!
This birthday seems to have come even more quickly
than the last, and that makes me wonder
if I am paying enough attention to my life,
to you, and what you are doing in me and in the world.
O God, if you can't slow the calendar,
at least slow me down!
Open my eyes to the daily miracles
that are always part of the journey with you.
Help me to "number my days"* not by fretting about
how many I've had and will have but by pausing often
to look for the goodness in my life and to give thanks
      for it.
Thank you for bringing me to this day.
Thank you for giving me life.
Help me honor your gift by living every moment fully,
including this birthday. *Amen.*

See Psalm 90:12, NIV.

On Turning Sixty

Gracious God, today I am sixty.
Now—no matter how I look at it—
I have fewer years before me than behind me.
Help me at this time of life to rejoice in all that has been
and to look forward to all that will be.
Guide my thoughts and actions in a way that keeps me
attentive to my role as one of your beloved children.
Help me to remember that my life is still filled with
opportunities to serve,
with people to love, with new places to explore.
Remind me too that because we are created in
your image,
we continue to have your creative spirit within us
through all the days of our lives.
Keep me excited about what there is to learn.
Let me be mindful of the need to slow down and notice
your Spirit
in the world around me and in the people I meet.

For all that has been and for all that will be,
I give you thanks. *Amen.*

A Prayer at Retirement

Great God of the ages,
I have worked for many years,
and now I am on the brink of retirement.
I'm excited and nervous, anticipating this new phase
and feeling qualms about all the adjustments.
As I approach this milestone,
keep my focus on the day before me
and relieve my anxiety about my last day of work.
Help me to complete with excellence the tasks at hand,
mindful of the legacy I will leave.
Strengthen me to live these days
as a good and faithful employee,
but even more as a good and faithful servant in
        your kingdom.
May I remain open to whatever new adventures
you have in store for me. *Amen.*

For a New Year

Gracious God, as this year draws to a close,
I am pensive about the year that is ending
and curious and hopeful about the year ahead.
O God, I need your wisdom and your guidance.
As I look back on this year,
I remember good things that happened. *(pause)*
I remember hard things I dealt with. *(pause)*
I celebrate those who helped and supported me. *(pause)*
I forgive those who hurt or disappointed me. *(pause)*
I give thanks for the chance to start over with a
        new year.
As I remember how I grew and changed this past year,
I thank you for being with me in my accomplishments
        and in my disappointments.
Whether I feel far from you or close to you,
I ask your guiding strength as I ease into the new year,
        loving God.
In Christ's name. *Amen.*

When Starting Something New

Creator God, I'm starting something new.
This time is filled with hope and dreams—
and a little bit of anxiety.
I want to do things right,
and I'm afraid I won't know how.

But you are a God who is always doing a new thing.*
Guide me, inspire me, shine through me.
Help me to remember that I am made in your image,
the image of a creative being.
Thank you for your presence
as I move into this new adventure. *Amen.*

See Isaiah 43:19.

The
Cry
FOR
Justice

For the Well-being of the City

*But seek the welfare of the city . . . for in its welfare you
will find your welfare. (Jeremiah 29:7)*

O God, we confess our need to be more diligent
in seeking the welfare of the city.
In our churches we often feel completely set apart
from the life of the communities that surround
     our buildings.
Open our eyes to the towns, boroughs, and cities,
to see the spiritual, social, emotional, and
     economic conditions
of the people where we live and worship.
Enable us to see and care about their struggles
and to hear their cries for mercy.
Give us courage to extend a hand,
lend a shoulder of support, and share our faith.
For as the prophet said,
our own well-being is entwined
with the well-being of those around us. *Amen.*

A Prayer for the Poor*

Jesus, you said that the poor
would be with us always—and they are here.
On street corners in blistering heat and in tent cities.
They are here—
women and children,
young folks and old,
some displaced suddenly,
others who slid slowly into the abyss
that hides them from us.

Here they are, Jesus,
hungry and thirsty,
in need of a doctor and a bath,
living in desperation in a land of plenty,
ragged and *shoeless* but criticized
for not pulling themselves up by their *bootstraps*.

Wake us to their humanity, O God,
and shift our eyes from "us" and "mine"
to these who are *thine*. *Amen.*

*Based on Luke 16:19-31.

For Those Abused and Forgotten*

O God, we pray for little boys given live ammunition and forced to fight wars that someone else started. We pray for little girls who are dressed up and painted up as women of pleasure. We pray for children who must work their way through childhood without play.

We pray for released ex-offenders with no safe place to go—not even the church. We pray for those trapped in prostitution and for those addicted to them. We pray for every person who suffers in silence with an addiction, or an HIV diagnosis, or a heart-wounding secret that can never be told.

We pray for the weak and sick and elderly who live without love and without loving, daily care. Lord, have mercy on the exploited and suffering peoples of the world, and have mercy on all who have lost hope.

And also, Lord, have mercy on us and forgive us for turning our eyes from all of this, pretending not to notice. Forgive us, Lord, for our complicity in these evils by remaining silent, for not acting on behalf of those in harm's way. Help us to remember that you

anoint your people to bring good news to the poor,
to proclaim release to the captives, and to help those
oppressd to go free. And help us to remember that *we*
are your people, called to lift our voices for the voiceless.

Give us perseverance to pray and fast, to work and hope
until women and girls, men and boys everywhere are
able to live in peace. In the strength and spirit of Christ
we pray. *Amen.*

Based on Luke 4:18.

A Prayer for Persecuted Christians*

God, you know the plight of people far away
oppressed by governments and vigilantes
in places where Christianity is an unpopular choice.

God, you knew that the day would come *here*
when truth telling would be despised,
and siding with the oppressed would be
the road less traveled.

Have mercy, O God, on followers of Christ
there and here who suffer harsh consequences
for speaking your name in word or in deed,
in defiance or in advocacy.
Grant courage and strength to all who would dare
to live their convictions out loud. *Amen.*

Based on Luke 21:12.

For Those Who Have No Voice*

Often no one speaks out for them, O Lord—
the ones who work at jobs that don't pay enough
to feed a family and pay the rent,
the single moms who struggle without child support,
the addicts who have lost everything.
The elderly who can't afford the medicines they need,
those beaten down who have lost jobs and dreams.
And all the other lonely and invisible people
whom we so easily forget, who have no voice.

We criticize for lack of ambition or education
ones whose worlds are so small they can't imagine
anything more or different than what they have.
Open our eyes and hearts to them.

O God, give us the will to speak up for those
who have no one else to speak for them.
Help us to cry out and keep crying out
until your ways reign in our cities and towns.
In the name of Jesus, who came to free us and them.
Amen.

*Based on Proverbs 31:8-9.

For Our Hurting World

O God, Creator and Redeemer,
I bring before you this world you so lovingly made.
Forgive us for the ways we have turned our backs
on you and on one another.
Have mercy on us, O Lord. Have mercy on us.

Everywhere we see examples of our inhumanity—
wars, terrorism, cruelty toward the weak and powerless,
hatred between countries, our own lack of response
to the needs right in front of us.

God, we pray especially today for the people of _____.
We pray for the leaders of our country and of
    all countries
as they make decisions that will affect the world.
O God, watch over us, your children, so that we
will turn to you for the peace only you can bring.
And help each of us to remember our responsibility
to love, pray for, and reach out to all people—
not just those we love but also those we call enemies.

Lord, have mercy on us. Have mercy on us all. *Amen.*

Loss

AND

Grief

At a Sudden Death

Gracious and loving God,
you know our hearts are broken,
heavy with grief and dismay.
This death is tragic,
and I imagine that you are crying too.
I know you don't want to see your children hurting.
Help us be kind and gentle with each other as we grieve,
and make us living reminders of you in the ways
we stand with the people we care about
who are suffering this loss.
Stop us from trying to explain the unexplainable.
Comfort those weighed down by sadness
and support them as they grieve.
In the name of Christ,
the man of sorrows and our hope of resurrection. *Amen.*

For Friends Grieving a Death

O God, my heart aches today for my friends
who are facing the death of one they loved so much.
Please be with them.
Give them your peace.
Help them to value their grief as a reminder
of the love they shared with the one who is gone.
May they find wholeness again, gradually and gently,
graciously allowing time to let you mend the hole in
their hearts.
May they know that you walk with them. *Amen.*

For One in Grief

Jesus, I remember the story of how you wept
in Bethany, seeing Mary and Martha's grief
over the death of their brother, Lazarus.
You know the wound of losing someone you love.

Precious Lord, I pray for _____,
whose heart must surely be breaking over this death.
Lord, wrap your loving arms around him.
Let him feel your comfort and presence.

Help me to be a friend during this time of sorrow
and in the difficult days still to come.
When I don't know what to say,
remind me that Job's friends helped
by sitting with him in silence.

Give my friend strength in times when it seems
he cannot make it through the day.
Balm of Gilead, bring your healing
to this wounded heart. *Amen.*

When Tears Blind Us

Loving God, we know that we can't escape
the suffering that comes with loss.
Even when we know loss is coming,
grief encompasses us.
A deep disappointment, a divorce, death—
each brings emptiness, loneliness, and sadness.
But you are with us to support us
when we think we can't go on.

You bring into our life
those who help us sense your presence
when tears and grief blind us.
Help us to trust that your everlasting love will guide us
as we walk through this dark valley of loss and grief
and that we will emerge into
the brightness of understanding and peace. *Amen.*

Alone with a Broken Heart

God, have mercy on me.
My heart is breaking.
I am drowning in my tears.
I feel so sad, so empty.
I don't know how to get through this.
I know that loss is a part of life,
but this feels so wrong.
People say that you are present with me,
but I don't feel you.
Have mercy on me, O God.
I need you. *Amen.*

The Loss of a Pet

Loving God, I know you care deeply for your creation,
humans and animals alike.
My constant companion has died—
the one who greeted me each day,
who kept a watchful eye on me at all times,
who brought easy joy into my life.
I didn't know losing an animal could hurt this much,
reminding me of other losses I have suffered.
I'm tempted to harden my wounded heart
to stand guard against more pain.
But instead I'm asking for your peace today.
Remind me of those things I've forgotten because
     of my pain—
the sweetness of your comfort, the safety of your love.
Keep my heart responsive to your tenderness and care.
Amen.

When Dreams Don't Come True

God, I have been wishing, hoping, and longing for
     something to happen.
That has created an empty space in me,
and I keep waiting for that space to be filled.
It is readily filled with disappointment,
doubt, and simmering anger.

What are my options, God? Do I give up? Do I
     move on?
Do I let that wishing, hoping, and longing shrivel
     into nothing?
I've heard that your grace is enough, that it is sufficient.
I don't know how to fill that space with grace.
I don't know how to turn my wishing and hoping
     and longing
into wishing and hoping and longing for you.
Show me how, Lord.
Fill that space with you, more of you. *Amen.*

I<small>N</small>
Uncertain
Times

Waiting for a Diagnosis

How long, O Lord?
I fear bad news,
but I am struggling almost as much with the wait.
You have seen me through the poking, prodding,
        sticking, and scanning; now I just wait.
Surely the doctors know my anxiety;
how can they make me wait?
I know—lab work has to be done, cultures have to
        grow, tests must be evaluated.
But why can't they do it now so I don't have to wait?

O God of infinite patience,
surround me with peace in this uncertain time.
Help me to remember that you are with me, no
        matter what.
Comfort those who worry for and with me
and assure them that their support, so freely offered, is
        "doing something."
In this awkward interim and in whatever may come,
I know that you are the great Healer.
I wait for you, and I know you wait with me. *Amen.*

Stress on the Job

God of wisdom,
Sometimes this place is chaotic and unpredictable.
Sometimes I am surprised by unforeseen changes.
Sometimes the systems and processes don't work as
    they should.

Sometimes I don't agree with decisions made by others.
Sometimes my colleagues don't complete their
    assignments; and sometimes I don't complete mine.

We are structured and restructured.
We worry that our positions will be eliminated.
We worry that we will disappoint others by the work we
    do or don't do.

I know that jobs always bring challenges.
And I know these challenges are potentially rewarding.
I am grateful for talented colleagues to work with
and for meaningful work to do.
Gracious God, I ask for wisdom, guidance,
and the strength to deal with what comes my way.
In Christ's name. *Amen.*

When Work Becomes Chaotic

God, it feels topsy-turvy here.
Each day when I arrive feeling ready to face the day,
entering my office throws all that readiness askew.
Waves of questions overtake me, and I ask myself,
When did work become chaos?

How could our leader have made that choice?
Can I trust those leading me?
Will the relentless push for change ever stop?
Will work ever feel energizing again?

Then your voice rises above the tumult: *Peace. Be still.*
And I remember.
I remember that you stilled storms, stopped waves,
and brought peace with just a word.
Your presence will still these workplace storms.
Your presence will calm the tumult caused by waves
    of change.
Your presence will bring peace with just a word.
Help me to remember that, O Lord. *Amen.*

Upheaval in the Workplace

God of the wind and storm,
I feel as if I am walking on troubled waters and about
    to sink.
The turmoil at work rolls around me,
pulling me in a destructive downward spiral.
I kick against it, which makes it worse.
I commiserate with colleagues, but this provides
    false relief.
I threaten to quit, which is irresponsible and foolish.
I hunker down with my work, and it brings only
    brief satisfaction.
I know that there is respite only in you.
You, who can calm the churning waters with a word
    or gesture,
help me to keep my eye on what is good and right;
help me to lend my voice to what is uplifting;
help me to keep my actions centered on what is fair
    and productive.
In all things, let me live and work as a witness to Christ,
in whose name I pray. *Amen.*

When Jobs Are Lost

Eternal God, things are changing.
At work, friends are losing jobs
and spending months without a new position.
They are struggling to maintain a home
and put food on the table.
They feel embarrassed because they need to ask
    for help—
something they never had to do before.
May I be aware of their needs.
Guide me to help them physically and spiritually during
    these trying times.
Let them feel your loving hand in theirs
as they walk this uncertain path. *Amen.*

When the Bills Pile Up

Gracious God, giver of all gifts,
I am overwhelmed by mounting bills
and dreading the times when they come due.
I am fearful of the late fees
and intimidated by the interest charges.
The weight of the debt is not the only problem;
I also face the judgment of others:
"It's your own fault." "Work harder."
Or glib comments:
"It will get better soon." "Get a different job."
Lord, lead me to what guidance is at hand.
Heal my pride so that I can ask for and receive help.
Fill me with peace and clarity that will enable me
     to see options.
Grant me the courage to trust you completely
and to find hope in your abundance and generosity.
Amen.

In Times of Financial Strain

Almighty God,
I feel powerless about my financial situation.
Every month it seems unexpected expenses arise,
and I have to scramble to find money to cover them.

Thank you for providing for me thus far.
I'm grateful to have a job.
I just wish, Lord, that the money would stretch
        a little further.

Your word says that you love a cheerful giver.*
And the Lord's Prayer tells us to ask for our daily bread.
Lord, is it wrong to ask for just a little more money
to cover all the bills, to give to the poor
and to my church, and to save for a rainy day?

Dear God, help me remember that it's all your money.
Show me how to live more simply
in order to share what I can with those in need.
Help me always to trust your generous heart. *Amen.*

*See 2 Corinthians 9:7.

In Threatening Weather

Almighty God, the storm clouds are ugly tonight.
Please keep all of us safe, alert,
and ready to heed the warnings.
Guard and protect your creatures,
especially those without shelter.
Keep us safe to see the promise and hope of
    a new morning.
Thank you for your love and care. *Amen.*

In the Face of Disaster

Lord God, we don't know how to pray.
This immense disaster feels overwhelming.
We can only imagine how the victims feel,
and we are so many miles away that we feel helpless.
Surround those directly involved with your loving
    presence.
Comfort the families of the dead and injured,
Sustain those waiting for word of those they love.
Protect, strengthen, and uphold
the rescuers and emergency personnel.
Help all of us to remember that your love
is bigger and stronger than despair and destruction.
Guide and strengthen us to reach out to those affected
in ways that will bring healing.
Give them and us a sense of your peace and hope.
In the name of Jesus, our friend and healer. *Amen.*

When World Events Seem Crazy

God, the world seems crazy right now.
It's frightening how many things are going wrong:
wars, natural disasters, economic crises.
We see suffering all around.
I worry for my friends and family,
for our safety, for job security.
I worry about our earth, what is going to happen next.
Help me remember that you are present in every
circumstance, with every being in distress.
Quiet my fears and enable me to take action
to be your hands and heart in this hurting world. *Amen.*

Awake in the Middle of the Night

Well, here we are again, Lord Jesus.
It's the middle of the night, and I am awake.
Have you awakened me,
or is my own anxiety keeping me awake?

You must have been awake some nights too—
the scriptures say you went into the hills to pray.*
I have tried to pray, but my mind wanders.

Help me to relax and not fret about this sleeplessness
and to let you guide me in my mental wanderings
toward clarity of your purposes
and what you are calling me to do.
Teach me to listen more carefully and to trust you more
　　fully. *Amen.*

*See Matthew 14:23.

To Love Truth

Teach us to love truth, God,
the unfolding truth that makes us know
who you are,
what kind of people
you want us to be,
and our purpose on this earth.

Tether us to truth, O God, and hold us steady
when the winds of doubt and confusion blow. *Amen.*

Asking

FOR

Healing

~

For My Own Healing

Loving God, I'm afraid.
My body is sick, and everything feels out of control.
I don't know what is wrong or what is going to happen.
I feel so alone, even with people all around me.
Help me trust the doctors who are working with me.
But mostly, help me trust you.
Whatever happens, I am yours.
Guide me to remember that whatever may come,
you will be with me, wrapping me in your love.
Thank you, God. *Amen.*

An Intercessory Prayer for Healing

O God,
here is my sister—
overwhelmed with grief and pain,
tearfully seeking your healing love.

Here is my brother—
anxious, lonely, and frightened—
uncertain even how to pray.
Do not pass them by, Lord Jesus.

Shine the light of your redeeming grace upon them.
Help them to feel your loving embrace.
Comfort them in their grief and heal their infirmities;
lead them in your way of love.
By the power of your Holy Spirit I pray. *Amen.*

For Healing in Suffering

Into your loving arms, O God,
I entrust my deepest needs, my strongest hopes,
and my greatest fears.
Grant me peace in my time of grief
and a voice that I might cry out to you.
Give me words to say what is most on my heart
and courage to seek the healing you have to give.
May I always offer my suffering to you
so that when healing does come,
wisdom, justice, and compassion may be its fruit,
in a life given to you, Abba God. *Amen.*

To Be Patient with My Body

Gracious and loving God,
sometimes my body disappoints me.
It is more vulnerable to illness than I think it should be.
It doesn't heal as quickly as I want it to.
A frightening diagnosis could mean
long-term treatment or surgery or both.
O God, please help me be patient with my body,
with how it responds or how it doesn't respond.
When my body disappoints me, I need your help.
I can't handle my feelings without you.
I ask for your presence and your wisdom
so I can face whatever comes.
May I find strength in you even when my body is weak.
Amen.

A Friend Is Seriously Ill

God, you've made our bodies so intricate!
It's fascinating—all these bones and muscles
and wondrous systems working together.
It's amazing that they don't go wrong more often,
but sometimes they do.
And something has gone wrong with my friend's body.
She has been diagnosed with a serious illness.
I don't know what to do. I don't want her to die.
I'm afraid.

While she lives in the midst of sickness,
fill her with courage and peace.
Give wisdom to the two of us
and to those who want to help her heal.
Strengthen our friendship
and let her sense your presence as she walks this path.

Thank you for our bodies.
Make us patient with the healing process,
        wherever it leads.
And thank you for being with us. *Amen.*

When Death Comes Slowly

Dear God, we ask for the touch of your grace
upon this person we care about.
As she draws nearer to eternity, grant peace.
With each breath, help her let go
of any anxiety that may burden these hours.
If concerns about beloved people or things undone
hold her here in the place between life and death,
work deep within to bring release and freedom.
Let forgiveness bridge any gaps that may trouble.
Let good-byes be said wherever they are needed.
If there is fear, heal it by your loving embrace.
Where there is pain, bring ease and comfort.

And, Lord, we ask your grace for ourselves too,
because this long death seems cruel.
As the lingering continues and we keep watch,
words about your kindness and tenderness seem hollow.
Help us to remember that your power extends
beyond what we see and beyond what we can explain.
Where we see suffering, remind us that your loving-
kindness goes deeper than we can ever know.
Shepherd of our souls, guide and comfort us all. *Amen.*

As a Child Dies

Dear God, I don't understand
why this child is dying while so many others live.
I keep praying for a miracle,
but she just gets sicker by the day.
I'm trying to understand how you answer prayers.

I believe that you do, but I don't see my prayers
    being answered.
Do I just not "get it?"
Or have all of us who are praying done something to
    offend you?

Even still I keep praying.
I really need to understand
why this child is dying while so many others live.
I could quit praying, but I just won't do that.
I want to trust you.
Help me with my lack of trust
and my inability to understand. *Amen.*

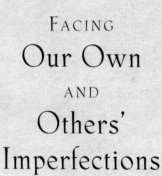

FACING

Our Own

AND

Others'
Imperfections

In Times of Temptation

God of infinite patience,
your love and care surround us constantly.
You know our hearts and thoughts
before we come to you.
You know our weaknesses of body, mind, and spirit.
You know our bad habits.
We trick ourselves into thinking that nobody sees the
wrong we do,
that we are hurting no one.
Yet we are hurting ourselves, your creation.

Shine your light into the dark areas we want to hide,
that we may see your love and your grace clearly.
When we face temptation, give us the strength
to say no to that which may harm us and others.
Help us to choose today, moment by moment,
to follow you.
In Jesus' name we pray. *Amen.*

When We Fail to Act

Dear God,
every morning I pass a poor man
who sells newspapers on the corner.
Sometimes I stop to buy a paper,
but most mornings I just drive by.
His face and his daily wave haunt me.
I want to help him and so many others who are poor.
My single dollar doesn't seem to be enough
in the face of his poverty.
Help me, O God, to get out of my car with the courage
to encounter this man and others like him.
Help me to find ways to respond,
to do more than pass by
or occasionally stop to give a dollar. *Amen.*

For More Generous Hearts

O God, we are ashamed to confess
that we have turned our faces from the sight of the poor
and have closed our hearts to their needs.
People in need are all around us,
and many are merely one or two paychecks away
        from poverty.

Forgive us, O God,
for avoiding the poor and for criminalizing poverty.
Forgive us, O God,
for living with tight fists and closed hearts.
Forgive us, O God,
for neglecting to do good when it is in our power
        to help.

Forgive us, O God, and give us open hands and
        generous hearts. *Amen.*

After Hurtful Words Are Spoken

Loving God, I messed up.
I hurt someone—someone I care about.
I feel like such a failure.
I am disappointed in myself,
and I don't know how to fix what I've done.
Guide me, God, in admitting my mistakes
and seeking forgiveness from the person I hurt.
I pray that person is able to forgive.
Help me make amends to the one I have harmed.
I am yours, God, even when I fail to act like it. *Amen.*

Betrayal by a Friend

Betrayed . . . again . . . by a friend.
God, you know what this feels like.
The confusion, the hurt, the anger . . .
All compounded by the fact that
we're talking about what a *friend* did and said,
what a *friend* didn't say or do.
"I thought I knew her."
"I thought I could trust him."
"Now I see her for who she truly is."

God, you know these strong feelings:
hurt, bitterness, desire for revenge—and all the others.
In Christ you experienced all of our pain,
suffered because of it, died to change it.
Hold me now and heal me, O God!
Save me from lashing out like a hurt child.
Teach me to grieve, to lament, to listen . . .
and finally to love once more,
as an older, wiser, more compassionate person.
In the name of the risen Christ I pray. *Amen.*

For an Absent Father

Dear God, my loving Father,
thank you for your presence in my life.
In the absence of my biological father,
you became my true father.
You extended supporting arms
to embrace me in my times of loneliness.
In times of silent crying, you comforted me.
Because of your love and presence in my life, O God,
I am able to forgive my father
for not being a part of my life.
Now, O God, I release to you
all the pain his failings caused me.
I am free, and I am loved by you.
Thank you, O God, for all these gifts. *Amen.*

Shine Your Light into Us

Shine your searchlight on us, O God.
Shine it into our hearts until *we* see what lies within.
And when we see, help us not to shrink away from you
in horror of what we are capable of doing.
Let us instead run to you and fall at your feet,
thankful that we saw these things.

Shine your searchlight, O God,
into the deep recesses of our hearts, and heal us. *Amen.*

SPIRITUAL
Searching

~

When I Need Light

O God, the sky is dark today,
and I am feeling darkness inside as well.

I don't know what to do next.
You know the struggles in my life right now.
I have decisions to make, and I am unsure which one
    is right.
I have decisions to make, and I'm feeling scared
    and anxious.

Come beside me, Lord.
I need the assurance of your presence.
I need to know the sun will shine again.
I need your comfort and direction.

Be present to me, O God, as I face my struggles.
Shine light on this dark path. *Amen.*

In Times of Self-doubt

Dear God, the "doubting Thomas" keeps
    showing up—
doubts about my choices and decisions,
doubts about my abilities.
I find myself wondering why.
Why am I constantly questioning myself?
Is it because I feel inadequate, not good enough?
Do I think that people will disapprove of me?

Doubts and insecurities pervade my life,
and self-doubt often prevails.
But I know deep down inside myself that you see me
as someone who is good and doesn't need to question.
You see me as someone who can think for herself
and has the ability to be a strong, self-assured person.
Help me, God, to hold on to my faith in you
and to the faith you have in me—
faith to get me through the times of doubt
    and questioning.
Help me to see myself as you see me. *Amen.*

Feeling Abandoned by God*

Merciful God,
you are the one who understands me.
You know my ways, my paths, and my thoughts.
Lord, you knit me together.
You were present when I breathed my first breath;
you will be with me as I breathe my last breath.
You are the inescapable God.

But, Lord, where are you now?
My world is crashing,
and I feel the heaviness of loss and fear.
I am burdened by a world that I do not understand,
a world that does not understand me.
Is your Spirit with me?
Have you left me here to suffer alone?
But, God, you promised to never leave me.
Make your presence known to me.
Remind me that no matter how dark the depths of my
        heart, darkness is as light to you.
Remind me that nothing is too hard for you.
Remind me that you are here with me. *Amen.*

*Based on Psalm 139.

Impatience with God

I fidget. I futz. I fret.
In my mind I hear "tick, tick, tick."
Time races on toward its eternal destination—
without me.
Surely there's more to life than waiting;
surely I didn't sacrifice my best years for this.

Waste! What a waste this has been!
God, do you see this? God, do you care?
I strain to hear you breathing.
Whisper something to me—anything—
so I won't sit alone . . .
in the silence . . .

(*Months later*)

I sit. I stare.

I shush my anxious soul.
I'm becoming accustomed to the quiet.
Thank you, Lord, for teaching me patience. *Amen.*

I'm a Failure at Prayer

God, sometimes I feel like a failure at prayer.
I cannot concentrate or meditate
or open up space for you in my spirit.
Every opening I try to create for you
is quickly filled with worries and distractions.
I long for quiet meditation,
for a solid, peaceful connection with you.
Help me, loving God, to let go of my expectations
and accept what happens when I sit down to pray.
I long for you, O God. Please fill me. *Amen.*

Discerning the Right Choice

Days of searching, praying, questioning.
Conversations with friends, family.
Reading the Bible.
Silence.

I'm trying to listen; I need to hear from you.
God, I've been asked to make a very difficult choice.
Rather than let my ego decide, I thought I'd listen
     to you.
Someone called this process "discernment,"
but it's not working, God. Please talk to me!

I am in agony. All I hear is silence.
My prayers bounce off the ceiling.
The deadline is fast approaching.
I'll be forced to make a decision on my own.

When I stopped fighting and demanding,
your message hovered over me with clarity
like the air after a morning shower.
I knew what you wanted me to do.
It was a gift, and I thank you. *Amen*.

I'm Growing Old

It's me, Lord.
That person you created years ago.
I need you, here and now, Lord.
Fill this broken body with your Spirit.

I'm growing old, and it's painful.
My energy leaves me when I need it most.
Let me know that I am still of value to you,
and even in my weakness I can still help others.
Fill my cup, Lord.
Fill me with your love. *Amen.*

When I Doubt God

O God, I feel like a hypocrite.
Many would say I am if they knew what I think
and what I believe—or rather, don't.
Everyone else seems sure of what they believe.
But when I try to say the creeds or sing the hymns,
some of the phrases stick in my throat.
I can't bring myself to speak words that I don't believe
    are true.
When others say comforting things about trusting you,
knowing you are in charge,
and believing that everything is in your care,
I can't join them in their confidence.
I'm just too cynical. Or maybe too wounded.
Whatever it is, I feel separated from those around me
by my questions and my doubts.
About the only thing I can say I believe for sure today
is that, as the Bible says, you are love.
O God, help me to believe that I can entrust myself,
even with all my doubts,
to your unwavering, unending love. *Amen.*

Gratitude

FOR

Ordinary Miracles

For the Gift of Friends

O God of all, thank you for creating us
with the need for someone else to know us and love us.

I am grateful for your love and for a relationship
with you but, loving God, I'm so glad that
you saw fit to create friends who understand me,
encourage me, laugh with me, and guide me.

I thank you today for my friends who have walked
with me in times of happiness and sorrow.

Thank you for _____ who knows just what to say
to cheer me up on days when I'm down.

Thank you for _____ whose jokes make me laugh
and lighten my spirit.

Thank you for _____ who senses when I'm lonely
and need to see a friendly face.

Dear God, thank you for these and all my friends.
Show me how to be a good friend to them as well.
Amen.

For a Friend across Years and Miles

Loving God, I want to tell you
how grateful I am for my Christian friend.
The connection between us grows stronger every day.
We may not talk often;
we may be hundreds of miles from each other,
but the wonder of how we are connected is a miracle.
Thank you.

We are so different yet so much alike.
We can pick up a conversation as if we spoke
 just yesterday.
I can call any time to say, "I need your prayers,"
or, "My family is struggling,
and I'm afraid we won't make it,"
knowing that she will be praying every day.
This is a gift, O God—a rare one!
Thank you for this wonderful bond
of faith and love and prayer that you have
created between us and sustained over the years. *Amen.*

To Be a Friend as Mine Have Been

Dear Lord, thank you for the women in my life.
Thank you for the mentors and friends who encourage,
    challenge, and embrace me on my journey.
Thank you for friends who have become like sisters
    who have shaped me and laughed with me.
Thank you for your love and care shown through them.
Thank you especially for my mother, for her strength
    and her care, for her love expressed and lived.

Dear Lord, thank you for the men in my life.
Thank you for the mentors and friends who strengthen,
    protect, and nurture me on my journey.
Thank you for friends who have become like brothers,
    who have taught me about solidarity and fun.
Thank you for your love and care shown through them.
Thank you especially for my father, for what I learned
    from him even when he wasn't aware he was
    teaching me.

O God, may I be your faithful follower.
And make me the kind of companion
for whom others give thanks. *Amen.*

For the Goodness in Every Day

Gracious God, thank you for the gift of this day.
We know that each day is a gift coming anew from you.
For the beauty of creation, we give you thanks.
For the joy of loving and being loved,
    we give you thanks.
For the steadfastness of good friends,
    we give you thanks.
For meaningful work to do and supportive colleagues,
    we give you thanks.
When challenges and hardships overwhelm us,
remind us that your grace is all around us, everywhere,
to be seen if we just remember to look for it.
Let our prayer at the end of this day and each day
be gratitude for what you have given to us.
In Christ's name we pray. *Amen.*

For Another Sunrise

I watch the sun rise and I think of you, loving God.
You, Creator of earth, the source of the sun,
the artist who paints colors in the clouds.
You, stirrer of the breeze,
voice of the mourning dove,
awakener of my soul.
My heart sings gratitude to you, creating God.
Thank you for another day. *Amen.*

A Morning Prayer

Loving God, thank you for the gifts you have already
    set before us to discover this day.
Our very life is a gift from you.

Forgive us our ongoing disobedience and sinfulness.
Amazingly, despite our sins, you persist with us.
You continue to shower us with your love, your grace,
    and your gifts.
Help us today to recognize these gifts.
And give us strength and wisdom to use them for
    your purposes.
By the Holy Spirit, empower, energize, educate, and
encourage us in the work we will undertake this day.

Watch over us and bring all of us home safely
    this evening.
Be with our family members, our friends,
    our loved ones.
Give them a sense of your presence in their lives
    this day.
We ask these things in the name of your Son,
    Jesus Christ. *Amen.*

In Praise of Ordinary Days

O God, today has been a good day.
I want to thank you for it.
So often it seems I come running to you
only with my problems.
But today I enjoyed blue sky and sunshine.
I walked with friends and enjoyed being outdoors.
People at work brought treats to share.
I enjoyed dinner at home with people I love.
We laughed together.

On the surface, it was just an ordinary day.
But throughout it I caught glimpses of you.
Thank you, God, for ordinary days like this one
that so often I fail to notice for their goodness.
God, you are so good. *Amen.*

For Loving and Being Loved

Most loving God,
of all your gifts, the greatest is love.
What a treasure it is!
We love imperfectly—sometimes selfishly,
sometimes generously, sometimes not at all.
Yet your love for me never fails.
Others find their ways to love me well;
I am blessed to love them in return.

Help me to know the depth and breadth
of your radical, unselfish love and to share it freely,
not only with my dear ones
but also with the stranger and the enemy.
As the unmerited recipient of your unending love,
I pray that my love may join yours in transforming
the stranger and enemy into neighbor and friend. *Amen.*

Thanks for Small Wonders

Dear God, small wonders and big surprises
remind me of your presence.
They amaze me and take my breath away.
They appear when I need to know you are with me.
When I see a ray of light piercing a hole in the clouds,
I remember that your love pierces our darkest days.
When I see a flower standing in a crack in the concrete,
I remember that you can create beauty in any situation.
These surprises are strong reminders
that you are with us in many ways, every day.
Thank you, God.
Thank you for being with me when I need you—
which is all the time. *Amen.*

Why Are You Mindful of Us?

O God, why are you mindful of us?
We cannot soar like the eagle or sing like the lark.
We cannot comprehend the breadth of the universe
or the depth of what it means to be infinite.

O God, why are you mindful of us?
We are on this earth for only the blink of an eye
when compared to the age of creation.
We are infinitesimal when considered
in the grand scheme of all that has been, is, and will be.

O God, why are you mindful of us?
We cannot explain the mystery of birth, life, or death.
We cannot give you anything that you do not
    already possess.

O God, why are you mindful of us?
Is it because you have created us for a special purpose?
Or because you are love, and you desire to love and
    be loved?
Help us to love you as you love us.
Let us rejoice, knowing that we are your children. *Amen.*

The Colors of Creation

Gracious God, the colors of creation
constantly remind us of the rhythm of life.
Your golden sun greets us each morning with the
     promise of a new day.
Your green fields proclaim the bounty that the
     earth provides.
Your gray clouds remind us of our dependence on the
     water that is necessary for life.
Your white snow covering the ground assures us of new
     beginnings.
Your orange sunsets cause us to reflect upon the passing
     of the day.
Your black night stills us so that we may have a time
     of rest.

O God, you have painted a glorious tapestry
     in each day.
We experience the beauty of your handiwork,
and our hearts overflow with wonder at your creation.
Amen.

For God's Unfailing Grace

God, we give you thanks for the grace
that lies at the heart of our faith.
Even as we fall short in our response
to your love and your call, your grace still abounds.
We see your grace in the sunlight that warms the earth
and in the stars that light the sky.
We see it in the manger at Bethlehem
and the cross of Calvary.
In your grace we find peace and healing
for troubled lives.
In your grace we see promise for justice and mercy
in a troubled world.
As you envelop us, enliven us, and embrace us,
we celebrate you as the God of grace. *Amen.*

Watched Over through the Night

Omnipotent God, while we sleep,
your work in the world and in our lives continues.
In the stillness of the night, without fanfare or fireworks,
your creative work goes on.
Thank you for being ever attentive,
for offering us a life absent of worry about tomorrow.*
Thank you for your grace that is more than sufficient.

We see you at work in nature
and in simple and lavish acts of kindness
extended from one person to another.
Your goodness is all around us,
beyond our sight and imagination,
never ceasing or sleeping.
Help us to let go of our anxiousness
and relax in the wonder of knowing you. *Amen.*

See Matthew 6:25-34.

God Who Deserves Our Praise

Gracious God,
my heart is filled with praise too deep for words.
Saying thank you is not enough.
In this rare moment when I quiet myself and give my
    attention to you,
I am aware that my breath is a gift.
The beating of my heart is a gift.
The ability to move and speak and think and sing—
    all are gifts.
O God, I am grateful for the mystery
of your love, grace, and generosity
toward an ordinary person like me.
"Thank you" is not enough.
Yet in the name of your Son, my Savior, Jesus Christ,
receive my worship; accept my thanks, gratitude,
    and praise.
Thank you. Thank you. Thank you. *Amen.*

For God's Love

Your love amazes me, O God!
How can it be that you, Creator of the universe,
are mindful of me?
I bow before this mystery and offer you my praise.

How can it be that the infinite God
could be limited to enter into a mother's womb—
incomprehensibly made human?
I bow before this mystery and worship and adore.

The promised Spirit, heavenly dove, descended on
Jesus—and on me.
You have spoken to us both:
"You are my beloved, in whom I am well pleased."*
Amazing love! Who can explain this mystery?
Yet, Lord, I believe.
In faith I bow before you to offer
all my worship, all my praise, and all my love. *Amen.*

*See Matthew 3:17.

Thanksgiving for My Church

Dear Lord, thank you for my church
and for the people who are a part of it.
I'm grateful to be reminded each Sunday of
      who I want to be,
      who you want me to be, and
      who you want us to be together.

Continue to guide the pastor, other leaders, and each
      church member.
Keep us faithful to you and to the mission you have
      given us.
Help our lives better reflect your love, both as
      individuals and as a community.

I pray for courage and encouragement
for those who are starting new churches.
Let their lives show your love and caring
so that many people who need you will find you.

Help my living always be a credit to my church
and a sign of my faith in you. *Amen.*

Gratitude for Christian Friends

God, we've walked together for years now,
my companions in Christ and I.
Each week we've met and prayed,
shared grief, celebrated milestones,
grappled with the mysteries found in following Jesus.
Most of all, we've offered one another the gift
    of safe space.
In this space, I am not judged; I can be myself.
We welcome each other as we are.
Who would I be, God, without these
    wonderful companions?
Their words have shifted my thinking.
Their generosity has restored my faith.
Their love has turned a hardened heart tender.
Such a gift, these creations of yours!
Each one has a story unique, distinct.
Their stories reveal nuances of your nature:
your creativity, your playfulness, your generosity.
Through them you have wrapped your arms around me
    and promised to hold me tight.
Through them you have shown yourself gracious,
    kindhearted, patient, and safe.
For them I am deeply grateful. Thank you. *Amen.*

CONTRIBUTORS

Tom Albin
Sharon Conley
Lynne M. Deming
Joan Floyd
Safiyah Fosua
Melanie Gordon
Karen Greenwaldt
Jerry Haas
Cindy Helms
Diana Hynson
Kwasi Kena
Kathryn Kimball
Migdiel E. Pérez
Mary Jane Pierce Norton
Robin Pippin
Mary Lou Redding
Beth Richardson
Roland Rink
Susan Ruach
Renny Stoltz
Anne Trudel
Edna Vaughan

Other Titles of Interest
from Upper Room Books®